De.

I hop [barcode MW00978552] agement
in the readers of "Hearing God
over all the madness" Truly
without Gods Voice in our
everyday walk it will be
madness!

Thanking you for your
prayers and Well wishes in
this endeavor.

God Bless you

Yours

Allan Lewis
2006

Hearing God Over All the Madness

TRUSTING GOD FOR EVERYTHING

Allene Lewis

Bloomington, IN

Milton Keynes, UK

AuthorHouse™
1663 Liberty Drive, Suite 200
Bloomington, IN 47403
www.authorhouse.com
Phone: 1-800-839-8640

AuthorHouse™ *UK Ltd.*
500 Avebury Boulevard
Central Milton Keynes, MK9 2BE
www.authorhouse.co.uk
Phone: 08001974150

First published by AuthorHouse 4/18/2006

ISBN: 1-4259-2792-0 (sc)

Printed in the United States of America
Bloomington, Indiana

This book is printed on acid-free paper.

To contact author, write to Allenel@hotmail.com

Dedication

It is not often that one has the opportunity to pen a book and for that I cannot take any credit for what God has allowed to become a reality. With this opportunity I dedicate this book to many; one being my church family. Many people down through the years have in someway contributed life experiences that have made me a stronger, better person so to Second Mount Vernon Baptist Church East, Inc. I say thank you for the love you have shared with me over the more than 33 years. Each of us at some point in our less than perfects lives, are trying to hear God in all our situations. Through the many trials that come our way, God will often send his voice for guidance. From the mothers in the church to the youth, I have received much inspiration from each of you. I love you!

I also dedicate this book to the Pastors who have had an impact on my life: To Rev. C. J. Gresham my pastor during my youth; Rev. Frank Traylor, my pastor during my teen years; Rev. G.W. Baker, my pastor during my young adult years and to my present pastor, William Holmes Robinson of the Second Mt. Vernon Baptist Church East, Inc.

It is Pastor Robinson that has exemplified the spirit of excellence to which I believe God wants us to operate in. I have learned so much and have grown spiritually from this young man of God.

And finally, I dedicate this book to my husband, Deacon Cary Lewis Sr. I see him as a living connection to God. His faith and his quiet strength are the weapons to which a remarkable man of God adorns in his every-day walk. His leadership in the church and in our family exemplifies the God in him. From the first time I met him, I knew he would be my soul mate. I thank God for allowing this man of God to be my husband.

Acknowledgment

Thank you God for your wisdom! Without your inspiration there would be no point of beginning. To my loving parents Arthur and Sarah Barham, though they rest in God's arm, hardly a day doesn't go by that I do not think of them. To my twin sister Alice Stansberry and my one and only brother, Arthur C. Barham, I love you much and will always love you! To my Husband Cary; my souls mate. Your walk of faith allows me to see daily that a *"Godly walk"* is rewarding walk. Your unwavering patience and quiet expressions of love remains as fresh today as it did the first time I met you. Did you ever know you're my hero? To my children: Chandra Spicer, Cartrice Myers, Cary Lewis Jr. and Cassandra Lewis and their spouses, Robert Spicer, James Myers and Renita Chanell Lewis, I love you much! As you all begin your families I can see a pattern of what your father and I have tried to instill into you. I can see God working in your lives. Always love one another and never ever allow the love you have turn to hate and envy. Love your mates. Get to know God's voice and listen for God's direction in your lives. To our grandchildren, I love each of you for the little persons you are. You all are captured memories of your parents. You are our rewards given through your parents by way of God. I am truly blessed!

About the Author

A native of Atlanta Georgia married to Cary Lewis Sr.; the mother to four adult children and grandmother to six grandchildren.

An active member of Second Mount Vernon Baptist Church East, Inc., located at 230 Stovall Street S. E., Atlanta GA., under the Pastoral leadership William Holmes Robinson. As an active member of Second Mount Vernon Baptist Church, Allene serves in the following church ministries: the choir Ministry, Deaconess Ministry, Drama Ministry and Christian Education Ministry.

Has earned a degree in Business Administration, graduated Magna Cum Laude with a GPA 3.70 and is presently employed in a leading company.

Hobbies are singing, writing poems and plays and directing weddings.

It is a sincere desire that people who partake of the words in *Hearing God over All the Madness* that someone is touched and moved to yielding to God and finding a sweet peace as they surrender all to God.

Favorite scripture: Hebrews 11:1 *"Now, faith is the substance of things hoped for and the evidence of things not seen."*

Allene Lewis

From the Author

It was neither by chance nor coincidence that this book is being presented. I truly believe it is the favor of God that has allowed such an endeavor to manifest itself. It is my hope that in some way it will spark interest to the reader and give them the initiative to Hear God over All the Madness. The madness in the everyday life situations; be it in our homes, our work, our family and yes even in the church. It is madness present!

There are situations that we can change by applying the spiritual guidelines of God. If we profess to be Christians then why is it hard to Hear God over all the madness? God is speaking to us daily, but we lack the instinct to hear his voice. That instinct that was clear as a child; we must recapture that instinct. To help us we must hear the word, read the word and most definitely do the word.

We all have his listening ear within our reach. This book not only ministers to the reader but to the author.

What are the distractions that have caused the most spiritual to hush up and say nothing?

I have been moved from my comfort zone to speak out as God would have me. I cannot possess a spirit of fear. In our everyday walk, we hear on the news and read in our papers the chaotic reports. Clearly we are living in a world that appears to have gone completely mad. I am saddened for our children and our elderly. It is as if they no longer count. That is why the vicious unfeeling predators can prey upon our youth and elderly. Children are our future and we must protect them. The elderly are our link to our past, we must cherish them. They were the torch bearers of yester years and without them, we would not be!

I hope that this book will provoke thought. I hope it will inspire us to begin to speak up and be not afraid, for "God has not given us the spirit of fear." *"We must hear God over all the Madness!"*

Table of Contents

Introduction

We are living in a mean world. When the smallest child cannot be left alone in peace; we have parents, biological and given now putting their rage on to the innocent children. A child may have to fight off relatives who should be protecting not abusing. Everyday it seems a child has been raged upon. Either through direct violence or indirect; just being in the house with the madness. We who know the word must now start putting it into action. We profess our Christianity yet we somehow allow things to continue because we do not want to step out of our comfort zone. We must start being the advocates for the innocence. We must be not only hearers of the word but doers. We must go among the enemy and take back our sanity. We must truly get the "grandmother" and "grandfather" tenacity of the days gone by and start taking back what is rightfully ours. Remember that as a follower of

God, we do not possess the spirit of fear. The village needs us to raise the children. The village needs us to be a light. That torch in the darkness. We must seek to bring the wounded vessels to Christ. We must teach our daughters and sons how to handle their circumstances in a positive way. We must hear God over all of this madness. There are many voices, but in our hearing we will know God's voice. His voice is distinct and can be heard. We must clear our selfish minds and hear his voice before its too late.

※

The Awakening

One morning as I awakened to the sound of my favorite news radio station, the news reporter reported that the suspect being sought for a triple slaying in our city surrenders to authorities in Mississippi. What great news I thought! This person in his undaunted rage had taken the lives of three people and wounded two others. Of this five, one of the murdered was a 3 year old and the two who survived the slaughter were ages 6 and 10. What a cowardly thing to do.

This incident is unnerving. Who could be so hateful and strike out against such a sweet innocent little child ? After hearing that the suspect was caught I rejoiced; then I became sad in a way for the suspect. Should I have had such sadness for this madman?

From a Christian's view, "yes." While I do not like the deed he has done, I still had to have some compassion. I had to realize that he at some time in his life was a child. What made him choose rage? The reporter mentioned that he was age 27 a young man. What could possess him to encompass such an act of rage and hate? Not knowing his background other than he was not a stranger to the penal system I had to wonder, what had his young eyes seen as he was growing up? Was there a village keeper in his life? For that matter has he ever heard the voice of God over the madness within his life?

Then there was the report of the mother who was charged with beating her 8 year old son bloody with an iron and knife and locked him in a closet while she had the audacity to go to a dance club! This madness must stop!

It is a sad commentary that children are now considered burdens and are being treated worse than ever. Is that what the word of God meant in Matthew 24:19- *"And woe unto them that are with child, and to them that give suck in those days!"*

Examples of such acts are a result of selfish, insane minded people. I can remember as a child growing up in my family that we had love abound. There were our parents and grandparents, aunts and uncles who looked out for us. We were fed and clothed and *"just seen after"* by the entire family. The village keepers were raising us. Because of that, we were able to raise our kids, with values, hope, character and integrity. "No" was not a bad word in my household. Disciplinary actions were not seen as abuse,

but as a tool to reinforce why the consequences of misbe-
having leads to the outcome.

We are living in the days in which a child's welfare
and being is threatened because there is so much dysfunc-
tion. Children seem to be wiser and "street smart" even
before they begin to walk. Clearly one can observe how it
appears the children and parent role has reversed itself. It
is the parent who jumps when the child speaks. Too often
I have heard young mothers say they cannot handle their
little one. I have often seen how parenting today, is with
a tied hand. If you discipline your child with a "belt or
switch" that is abuse. If you do not discipline your child,
you end up with a wild, untamed child who may be destined for a committed jail sentence or an early grave.

It is unfortunate today that many children are looking
for the closeness and attention from their parents and are
not getting that much needed attention. Without that
common bond, it is easy for other entities to manipulate
and con the child out of their innocence. Even the trust
with a blood relative is questionable and could lead up to
darkness in these evil times. The deceiver uses the tactics
that a loving parent should use to gain trust. Once that
trust is established the line is crossed and with the all
too familiar phrase, *"don't tell nobody,"* or *"It's our little
game,"* thus another child becomes a statistic. Mothers
and fathers, you need to hear God over all this madness!

We must listen for the voice of God and do the right
thing in rearing our children. For it is written: Proverbs
22:6 *"Train up a child in the way he should go: and when he*

is old, he will not depart from it." To do less puts everyone in jeopardy.

Without a doubt the presence of the spirit of rage is alive and well but it does not have to be. There are people who realize they are in trouble and seek out help. It is written: Matthew *7:7 "Ask, and it shall be given you; seek, and ye shall find; knock, and it shall be opened unto you: For every one that asketh receiveth; and he that seeketh findeth; and to him that knocketh it shall be opened."* (King James Bible)

Now the time is come for those who are equipped through the teachings of the word of God to stir up and tell the lost souls; the unsure saints and sinners that all they need to do is ask! There is hope. If nothing else, call out! *"Have mercy on me!"* We who know Christ must assure the seeking they don't need money, fancy clothes and the comfort of plush pews and beautiful sanctuaries. Salvation is free! It does not just operate one day a week! It's not just confined to a four-wall structure! We, who profess God and have a working relationship with God must help the disillusioned and lead them to God.

Mark 10: 14-15
"But when Jesus saw it, he was much displeased, and said unto them, Suffer the little children to come unto me, and forbid them not: for of such is the kingdom of God. Verily I say unto you, Whosoever shall not receive the kingdom of God as a little child, he shall not enter therein."

When Is Enough, Enough?

When is enough, enough? What must God do to get our attention? It was during our June 2004, revival that our guest Minister, Rev. Dr. Steven Thurston, asked us *"What's in your mouth?"* Truly that reached deep within my heart. We who sit comfortably in the many worship services giving outright praise yet if the truth be told, at what point do we sound out what is right? Do we see and witness wrong doing and yet never speak up and say to the offender that is wrong what you are doing? I am guilty. When does watching and not speaking up becomes enough? Without a doubt we are witnessing a time in which people do not care about human life. There is a total disregard for one another. Children have made adults scared to walk down their streets. There is the fear factor that one or more kids together is a gang and the way they dress and talk and act, leaves little room to suspect nothing good coming from their gathering. When is enough, enough? Dr. Thurston brought out the points that from our mouths we have power. "Power to lift up or destroy." When we gossip we destroy. When we praise God and profess the work of Christianity we build up! As we seek out the voice of God, over all this madness, we must know what is in our mouth? When we hear the familiar passage from the book of Psalms," *I will bless the Lord at all times: his praise shall continually be in my mouth.*"

(Psalm 34:1 King James Version), we so candidly say this passage but do we honestly understand what it is saying? Are we good stewards with our mouths? We must with our mouths shout out enough! It is time to yell out stop! No more rage on our children. No more rage within our families and our communities. Crying out with passion will help us to hear God over this madness. We must take back what is ours. Yes we must go into the enemy's camp and take back what is ours. We must try and hear God over all this madness. *What's in your mouth?* I have looked in the mirror and have literally cried out to the Lord to use me. I am not perfect, nor do I profess perfection but I want God's perfect peace and to be in his will. I have to admit that when Dr. Thurston brought to us this word, he was talking directly to me. I know now that we all can talk the talk but it is walking the walk that matters. If we who profess a Christian life are walking in that life then no doubt we should be equally yoked in our actions, in our talk and in our entire being. It is then that we can speak out enough and have the power from God to carry out his will in our lives and others.

"1 Samuel 3:10
And the LORD came, and stood, and called as at other times, Samuel, Samuel. Then Samuel answered, speak; for thy servant heareth."

That Love That Reaches All

When I think of love, I do not just limit it to physical love like the touching, caressing and intimate moments. As a woman I thrive from that nurturing moment from my soul mate. But as a professed follower of God we must have that *agape* love. What is agape love? The American Heritage Dictionary defines it has, *"Christian Love; Love that is spiritual, not sexual in its nature."* This is the love that can reach into madness and salvage lives. I liken it to when I drive, I often see people in a situation for example they may have car trouble and are trying to attend to that problem. I whisper a prayer for them. I often see a person who has the appearance of someone who is homeless, if I cannot physically reach them, I certainly whisper a prayer for them right then. I pray that God will intercede on their behalf.

I am reminded of the day in which a young man decided that he was not going to be incarcerated, so he overpowered his deputies to whom he was being escorted by and in the process of his escape, he attacked a deputy injuring her in the head severely; he then made his way through the judges chamber onto the courtroom and with the deputy's weapon he shot and killed the judge and a court reporter; from there he made his escape onto the street, there he encountered another deputy and shot and killed that deputy; from all of the events it was chaos. While watching the television as these details were being broadcast, I was in shock that this could be happening. Not knowing this obviously deranged man's whereabouts was quite disturbing. As the night ended without his capture, I began to pray and ask God to please intervene and get this man off the streets. Many of the law enforcement teams thought by now he was long gone from our city. It had been last reported that this man had car jacked a vehicle. But little did we know he had yet murdered again and finally taken refuge in a woman's home, taking her as hostage. To make a long story short, agape love salvaged this situation. Here we see a woman who had a faith that puzzles the non-believers but reinforces to the believers what God is about. As she began to witness to her captor she reached out and showed love. No doubt in all this madness there had to have been praying saints. Through this entire ordeal, the woman did not have a spirit of fear; she chose to be the servant of God and seize the opportunity to save lives, hers and her captor. Agape love.

I found it such a coincidence that she was reading Rick Warren's book, "The Purpose Driven Life" to him. She was on Chapter 33, which was titled *"How Real Servants Act"* coincidentally the captor was "33 years old" profound isn't it? She truly followed what a servant's attitude was about, to serve. Sometimes we are put into servant situations that without the agape love we would perish. Like Joseph, even though his brothers somehow rid him into slavery, in spite of his situation he trusted God and maintained his agape love for his brothers. Even for his overseers. I must interject here, that my pastor has taught us so many times about being a willing follower, having a servant's attitude.

Matthew 10:42 reads, *"If you give even a cup of cold water to one of the least of my followers, you will surely be rewarded"* this was a key verse in that chapter and this woman, could have been the captors true ticket out of town, but she ministered to him to save herself and him. She did things that the non-believers cannot understand, and no doubt when the trial goes forward she will be asked and no doubt she will express her faith as she has in the media. Of course there was the pointing of fingers as to her real motive, *"the reward money."* I would like to interject my opinion, that if her motive was the money, I still say it was her agape love that tamed this young man enough to hear a word from God. Yes she did collect the reward money and frankly it was not enough, but the fact that her actions constrained this man and allowed his capture so he would no longer hurt anymore people or end up dead himself. After all he has a loving family that would surely need answers as to why he did what he did? The families of the victims are going to want to know why? So in Hearing God over all the madness we must be equipped with that love that reaches all, agape love.

1 John 4:9-10 KJV
"In this was manifested the love of God toward us, because that God sent his only begotten Son into the world, that we might live through him. Herein is love, not that we loved God, but that he loved us, and sent his Son to be the propitiation for our sins"

Leader or Follower— How Will You Know?

Often I have been told I make a good leader. While I do not mind leading I have to ask myself am I a good follower? While sitting under the awesome leadership of my pastor, he often teaches that in order to be a good leader one must first be a good follower. Too often especially in the church community people who are given authority as a group leader will mistake the position to be "lord over the people to whom they are leading." In some cases a *"bully."* It is unfortunate that this behavior has over flowed into the church. It is enough that while in the world these Pharaoh types are in our work places and one has to be subjugate to these tyrants (perhaps as we learn to hear God over the madness-we can make choices about our work environment) simply because we must work and think we cannot do better, therefore we find ourselves under the will of such people. In the church we should not have to tolerate such behavior. That is why it is important for pastors to be fully connected with the will of God for instructions in picking people to be over people. We depend on their leadership to guide us to Christ. It is no wonder that pastors are beginning to delegate task and duties to others so that they can fully be in the will of God. As a congregational member we must be willing to accept leadership if delegated by the pastor. We must see this as an extension of the pastor; therefore we must lead with humility and humbleness. In the same spirit we must be willing to follow leadership. Sure we all want to be wanted and needed but in this Christian walk some of us may never be leaders but followers and as a good follower you may not realize it, but that humble attitude of following may very well lead someone to Christ. Just think "if there were only leaders" we would never get anything accomplished. As we try to hear God over all the Madness, we must pray that Gods will direct us to be the leaders and followers we are destined to be. I am reminded of Ruth, how after the death of her husband, her mother in law Naomi, appealed to her and her sister in law to retreat to their own mother's house. Orpah, Ruth's sister in law wept in sorry, kissed Naomi and left. Yet Ruth, out of love that agape love chose to stay and said *"Intreat me not to leave thee, or return from following after thee: for whither thou goest, I will lodge, thy people will be my people and thy God my God"* (Ruth 2: 15-16) from this faithful follower came a lineage of greatness. If we trust God there is no doubt he will prepare you for leadership and he will equip you. Just ask Moses. He was a great example on hearing God and being used by God to lead.

ON LEADERSHIP

*"A leader is one who knows the way, goes
the way and shows the way."*
(Unknown)

*"A leader is one who sees more than others see, who sees
farther than others see, and who sees before others see. "*
(Leroy Eimes)

ON BEING A FOLLOWER OF CHRIST

*A follower has to be prepared to move both physically
and spiritually. One has to take on the humility of
servitude. Being a good follower is the stepping stone
toward being a good leader. An example of a follower
would be Joshua. Joshua had an unwavering loyalty
and devotion to Moses. It is this walk with Moses that
prepared him for leadership. Therefore if you want
to know if you are a good follower, study Joshua.*
(Allene Lewis)

In Season and Out of Season

Little did I imagine I would be in the condition I am in now; sure I have imagined at a later time as the Lord blesses me to age, I would not always have the health I exhibited in my earlier years. Now, here I am recovering from leg surgery and broken anklebones. I am not back to normal, but I can at least walk again. Thank you Jesus! But through this whole experience, I have found added strength. I must say, it came at a time at which I was beginning to be burned out from my job activities. I liked my job; I enjoyed the daily interaction with people of all walks. I would see it as an opportunity to let the Jesus in me shine and give strength to all I came in contact with, but there were some very stressful times and I look back now and truly believe God removed me from that environment because he could see a bigger picture than I. Who knows; I may have been heading for a stroke or a heart attack and since I was failing to hear God over that madness, God sat me down. Had I listened enough? Perhaps not, so once again God sat me down. One week pending my release from the doctor I fell and broke bones in my ankle. Okay God you got my attention. Now I was really incapacitated. I had an opportunity to be angry and frustrated but I didn't feel that. I knew it was an opportunity for God to make me hear him over all the madness. It was also an opportunity for bonding even more with my husband. I felt very humble and appreciated to having a very good and loving husband to take care of me. I thought of the marriage vows, the part where it says "in sickness and in health" truly my darling husband exemplified that to the fullest. I felt so pampered! During this time that God prepared for me, I have had some very serious quiet times with God. For one thing I have asked God to forgive me for everything that did not exemplify him. I know I am not perfect and God knows that too, so he takes the time to mold you and make you into a new being. He has asked me to put those imperfections into the sea of forgetfulness. During this special time with God, has given me instructions and I have committed myself to make sure that I follow those instructions. God allowed me to hear his voice during my time with him. I know he has allowed me to pour out in this book his will for me. I am guilty of not being faithful in my tithes. That is one area that I know God is telling me to be better in. Like many, I fall short in this area, but I am committed in bettering myself in this area.

I know that God is going to bless me to have the resources to be a committed giver. I cannot worry that I no longer have a job, I truly am believing God to supply me with something better. I am reminded of the widow who gave her all. *"Jesus saw the rich putting their gifts into the temple treasury. He also saw a poor widow put in two very small copper coins. "I tell you the truth," he said, 'this poor widow has put in more than all the others. All these people gave their gifts out of their wealth; but she out her poverty put in all she had to live on"* (Luke 21:1-4) We cannot make any excuse as it relates to our giving. If we want to exemplify utter devotion to God, giving is the area by which God asks us to try him and see.

I have had this quiet time to put into perspective what is important. These quiet moments have benefited me in more ways than I will ever be able to tell. As far as my job the facility has closed which resulted in me being laid off. I have concluded that God did not want me to go back to work at least not to that place. I am also trusting God to place me where he wants me to be. I know that he has a bigger plan for my life. I will not worry about the finances for God is the provider and he has taken good care of me and I know without a doubt he will continue to do so. I know I am being repetitive in this area of thought, but I know God prepares for his people a way out of no way. I hope that I can be used by God to inspire someone to never give up; to continue to look up for God is watching over us even when we are not worthy to be in his shadow.

God wants us to take on his likeness in season and out of season. In other words when things are going great or when things are going not so great we must continue to trust God; we must continue to pray. God does not want us to straddle the fence."*I know your works that you are neither cold nor hot; I could wish you were cold or hot. So then, because you are neither cold nor hot, I will spew you out of My mouth" (Revelation 3:16).* This passage refers to the churches and as professed Christians we are the church. In our daily lives we must not offend God; he will spew us out. I thank God for his will in guiding me closer to him in this way. *"I can do all things through Christ which strengthens me"* (Philippines 4:13) I can truly say that in season or out of season, God wants us to hear him over all the madness. God has a way of getting our attention. If you don't believe me ask the apostle Paul what happened to him on his way to Damascus? In his madness he was a persecutor of Christians. But one day as he was setting out to do what he thought he did best: intimidate, humiliate and incarcerate. But little did he know in a light brighter than all bright he would hear Gods voice. From that hearing of Gods voice one of God's greatest prophets was ordained.

Ecclesiastes 3:1
"To every thing there is a season, and a time
to every purpose under the heaven"
(King James Version)

Excuse Me World—But God Is Still in Control!

In this world today there are many that would question if God were real? How dare they! Can't they see even with all the madness of this world **God is real** and he is still with us? He said he would be with us. From the physical aspects, when we see the sunrise in the mornings or when the moon and stars light up the night sky, there is a God. When we see the birth of a child or inevitably when we experience the death of a love one or friend or in just reading the obituary that is God in control.

We are experiencing many unpredictable weather patterns. We have many conditions that even the media will phrase it as,*"biblical proportions."* I know I am grateful for God for sparing my family and me during these times. It seems when the weather is very threatening God encircles us and allow the storms to pass over.

When I think of the Tsunami that occurred recently in the Asian hemisphere, my heart hurt for all the sufferings we viewed via TV. We cannot explain why such devastation and destruction. No doubt God is sending nature into action to get the attention of this world. Granted we have to wonder if what happened there, could such destruction and devastation happen here in Atlanta?

A word from Matthew 24: 7-8, "*For nation shall rise against nation and kingdom against kingdom: and there shall be famines, and pestilence, and earthquakes, in divers places. All these are the beginning of sorrows.*"

I know God is sovereign and he can do what he wants to do, when he want to and how he wants to; so while it may not be a wave, it can be enough to get our attention. So Hearing God over all the madness, I will shout to the world, Excuse me, God is still in control! We cannot fear what man has placed in our thought either by TV, radio or any other media. We must get into our bibles and read for ourselves the word. Getting into the word of God will give us solace in times that might seem confusing and chaotic. Yes to a degree we will have fretful moments; we are human but studying and getting into God's word will enable us to understand why nature is speaking out thus freeing us from the spirit of fear. God protects his people and he warns us of the times to come. He is in control and therefore we will be able to hear God and strive toward his perfect will.

2 Timothy 2:4
Preach the word; be instant in season, out of season;
reprove, rebuke, exhort with all long suffering and
doctrine. (King James Version)

Patience—A Gift From God

As we grow older we tend to develop more patience. Not on our own, but by the grace of God. Patience is in my opinion one of the many important attributes a human being could have. I have to admit that only when I reached my forties did I start exemplifying patience. Before that point I had *"selected patience,"* meaning I only had patience with certain people and situations. When I think back I can only hope I didn't hurt anyone. Patience is a part of Love. It is the part that as a professed Christian, we must have and we must exemplify. If we can get back to the basics in which the churches preached about love and concern for each other there is no doubt that the wealth of problems that individuals and families are experiencing will become null and void. If we can use the fruit of the spirit as our guide as it relates to Christian relationships there would be such an awakening in our lives.

What are the fruits of the spirit? *Galations 5:22 -23 reads: "But the fruit of the Spirit is love, joy, peace, patience, kindness, goodness, faithfulness, gentleness, self-control; against such there is no law."* (Revised Standard Version)

In Gods plan for us to be in his will the fruits of the spirit is the key to opening the many doors that God has for us. "Now that we have the fruit of the spirit now what?" Galatians *5:24-25 reads: "And those who belong to Christ Jesus have crucified the flesh with its passions and desires. If we live by the Spirit, let us also walk by the Spirit."* (Revised Standard Version) The road map is laid. Understanding the word of God will enable the professed Christian to acquire the patience that sustains us in time of trouble and allows us to hear Gods voice over all the madness.

Gods Will Exemplified in Prayer and Healing

I can believe that being in Gods will is the first phase of peace within the spiritual body. Having been a person who has not lived an outrageous life; I didn't acquire a taste for the fast life that I hear people talk about being delivered from. Perhaps it was due to marrying and starting a family early. So I didn't have the little break time that most people have after graduating from high school. I guess I will never know because I have never regretted the life that God designed for me. I believe deep in my heart that if I had not gotten married, God's everlasting will would have been upon my life and I still would not have experienced any alternate lifestyle. I do know that early in my life I found Jesus. At the age of seven I remember joining the church and being baptized. I knew fully what I was doing. Even though I was a child, I was aware that God was with me early. I can attribute that to having a praying mother and father who in their wisdom would council and give instructions as we (my siblings and I) were growing up. I can remember when as a child we didn't have a TV and one of the things my mother would do is get us ready for bed then she would read the bible to us. We had a radio and she would let us listen to the music usually it was gospel music. As I think back it was good to see my parents pray and have the relationship they had with God. I even remember our grandmother and grandfather. They were loving and caring and it was always happy times being in their presence. God has been with me all of my life.

As a young child I could remember my sister Alice and I would go with our mother and the other women in the church to visit the sick and shut-ins. We would always close out the visit with a prayer and a song. It was a good feeling to know that we were able to cheer someone who was sick. It is that experience I feel has had a great impact on my life. That experience is what I believe helped mold me to be a concerned person for people who are sick and are in need. When God's will is with you it opens you to the opportunity to help and minister to people. I have to add here there is nothing so grand that I have done by myself that keeps me. God is the one responsible. I thank God for giving me an early foundation in knowing him; hearing his voice. Sometimes one has an opportunity to experience God early in life. I can never forget a time when my sister was diagnosed with cancer. This would have been in the early sixties and cancer was an extremely scary word to hear let alone the idea of it being a child's diagnoses. Only after I was older did my mother tell me all the details involved; under the recommendations of the family doctor, my parents began to make preparations to take my sister to Boston, MA. Upon my mother and sister's arrival to the children's hospital in Boston test were done to confirm the primary doctor's diagnoses. Within a day it was confirmed she had cancer. With that news the doctor's at Boston MA, began to outline the treatment procedures. I remember the emptiness I felt in not having my sister with me while under the care of my grandmother. It was very hard probably harder than most people experience, you see my sister and I are identical twins and we had never been apart. I remember saying a prayer for my sister and Mother while they were away. In a kids way I didn't know how serious things was and back then children were not privy to "grown-up stuff." I remember getting a post card with a cute little dog on it and my sister Alice had written me a note. I was so happy. Nonetheless the doctors at the hospital were to start treatments immediately. One thing they hadn't counted on was a praying mother. My mother setup camp around my sister's bed and began to call on Jesus. She must have been very animated because the hospital felt that my father should come up. Prior to my dad's arrival my mother said in all her praying it finally dawned on her that she no longer needed to worry. She began to acknowledge to God that it was okay to take my sister after all, he'd given her two, (our twin birth was a surprise to my mom and her doctor) and she had another child at home. It is after that affirmation and acknowledgment that my Mom knew Jesus had heard her cry. By then the doctors were ready to start the treatments and because of my sisters age and the location of the cancer, they wanted to do one more test to be on the safe side. Upon receiving those test results a miracle had occurred. The cancer that had been diagnosed and confirmed was GONE! The doctors were baffled and elated. Of course my parents were happy but my mother who knew that there was going to be a healing was not surprised. I am happy to acknowledge to date my sister is doing well. We often speak about that journey and conclude that there is something else left for Alice to do, so until then we know she will be all right. Just having that experience in my life was a way for God to allow me to see him in my mother's action. Having God's will upon your life is like knowing you always have the favor of God and when it comes to God's favor that is better than anything. Truly what God has for you it is for you.

It is his will
"When we awaken to each new morn,
it is God's will that we are kept
In his perfect peace and care throughout the day."
unknown

Reach Out

I am reminded on one occasion while I was at work, a young man walked in to utilize the services. He seemed a little distraught and dazed. I set-up the workstation and he began to type away. Somehow I could sense in my spirit that this young man was burdened down.

As he began to conclude his time at the workstation I was led to speak to him. I asked him was he okay and he said, yes. But then he began to tell me what was going on. He was trying to find a flight to the DC area. He was returning from over seas and had gotten word that his grandmother was very ill and there was a possibility she would be placed in a nursing facility. He had to find flights that would meet his budget. While he was speaking I could see the tears begin to wail up in his eyes. At that point I grabbed his hand and begin to pray for him and his grandmother. I thanked God for giving me the words to use. I knew he needed to hear of life and not death. We then embraced one another and I whispered to him that his grandmother was going to be fine and for him to be reminded that the bible tells us all sickness is not death. As I ended his transaction with a receipt, I was happy to give him a card so he could let me know how his Grandmother would be doing, for God gave me a word to tell him that his grandmother would be fine and for him not to worry. He thanked me and departed. I thank God for using me to reach out. In our mission statement at church, one of the lines is *"to reach out to those in need in both our local and global communities."* I truly take those words seriously. Every opportunity I had I reached out! I was fortunate to be in contact with many people of many backgrounds and status. It didn't matter that they were obviously of another race or religion, it was important that as God led me I was able to give them a word from the Lord. This was not of my doing but of God. I just thanked God for allowing me to know when to speak.

I have had many opportunities to share God and while all of them will always be special, there was one episode that truly blessed me. It was years ago on a Saturday, October Morning. My youngest daughter had to be downtown for a youth meeting so I decided since it was a pretty fair day we would ride the MARTA transit system. Upon our arrival at her meeting location I decided I would walk to the nearest eatery for breakfast and wait for the shops to open. As I was walking, I approached a gentleman in very raggedy and dirty clothes. He asked me for some money so he could get something to eat. I told him I didn't have any money but I would be back. I asked him to wait. He anxiously asked me if I was coming back? I guess he didn't believe me. I proceeded to the eatery. I asked for a full hot breakfast, so there was grits, eggs, bacon and so forth. I added coffee and Juice to the meal. I happened have the little booklet *"the Daily Bread."* I had some extra bus tokens. I bagged up the food and placed the religious booklet and tokens in the bag. I wanted to hurry back to the gentleman because it was getting ready to be busy downtown and no doubt the police would soon make the man leave since there is no loitering. I could see the man in the distance and I could tell he spotted me. I gave him the bag and he was so grateful. I asked him if I could sit down and talk with him. He seemed very happy for the company. He pulled out the little book and I told him there were some nice stories and scriptures that I thought he would like to read. I told him I didn't have any money but if he needed to catch the bus there were at least some tokens to do so. Again he was grateful. I asked him how did he get in the condition he was in? He began to share his story. He was a college graduate and was once a successful businessman. He'd had a family and house and cars. He'd started using drugs and the next thing he knew he had lost everything and his wife left him. He became homeless and he didn't have any family that would be bothered with him, so shelters and places all to familiar to the homeless community became his place to reside. I felt so moved from his story. I then asked him if I could pray with him. God gave me the prayer for him. Afterwards I needed to leave and get with my daughter, but I left a word with him. That word was no matter how difficult things got, just remember God loved him and he was never alone. He thanked me and I left. As I looked back I really felt blessed to have had the resources to share with that brother. I also think that the greatest gift that was given that day was the fact that I stopped to speak life and hope into a person who had nothing. I knew that it was only by the grace of God that that moment was given to me. I will forever cherish that feeling. I cannot remember the stranger's name but I know God knows his name.

I truly believe that God wants us as professed Christians to reach out and connect with the less fortunate. It is nothing so grand that I have done that makes me privilege and above such conditions. It is only by Gods grace and mercy that I am not in a similar situation.

I remember growing up there was a saying that simply said *" be careful how you treat a stranger, because you never know when you are entertaining an angel."* As I look back I think I did entertain an angel. I know I heard the voice of God over the madness. The madness for that moment was that of homelessness. I heard God's voice distinctly.

I can conclude that our blessings are tied up in Hearing God. For the wretched soul that is seeking to hear God over the madness in their lives I pray that they truly labor in prayer and supplication for God is right there in the midst. To rid one's self of the madness there must be a peaceful spirit. We who profess to be Christian's are commissioned to show the unhearing the way. God does not force himself, but he does freely give himself to all that hears his voice over the madness. The madness I speak of is anything that blocks out the good. If people are hurting be it in an abusive marriage, if it is an abusive parent toward a child, an uncaring caregiver to an aging parent. Be it a lifestyle that contradicts the very fabric of God's commandments; we must pray to hear God over all the madness. There is refuge in God's wonderful light. May God add a blessing to hearing of his word!

Poetic Words of Expressions

God has blessed me to put into written words my thoughts. Like most artistic expressions its beauty and understanding are like any art form; in the eye of the beholder its beauty is found. I pray that whoever partake of this book, "*Hearing God over all the Madness*" will find consolation and will find strength as well as food for thought. I know that I have been blessed from the reading of his word. It is my prayer that I grow stronger in the Lord. I know I can hear the voice of God and I love how he is with me day and night. This madness in our homes, church, schools, neighborhoods, jobs, our government and streets must stop! We must be equipped and ready for battle, for when God's voice is heard by all he will be coming back for us. We do not know the time or day, but we do know it is going to happen. 1 Thessalonians 4:13-17 (KJV) states:

[13]But I would not have you to be ignorant, brethren, concerning them which are asleep, that ye sorrow not, even as others which have no hope.

[14]For if we believe that Jesus died and rose again, even so them also which sleep in Jesus will God bring with him.

[15]For this we say unto you by the word of the Lord, that we which are alive and remain unto the coming of the Lord shall not prevent them which are asleep.

[16]For the Lord himself shall descend from heaven with a shout, with the voice of the archangel, and with the trump of God: and the dead in Christ shall rise first:

[17]Then we which are alive and remain shall be caught up together with them in the clouds, to meet the Lord in the air: and so shall we ever be with the Lord.

1 Thessalonians 4:13-17. (KJV)

The Following is a personal collection of poems I know were inspired by God. These expressions somehow relate to hearing God over all the madness. I will share with you my thoughts of each poem and how it was derived. I know that even as the world around us often times seems to crumble there is an outlet. Whether through reading or writing, singing and dancing, the creator has allowed us to release our self-expressions into these venues. If we are to have peace and joy, we must *"Hear God over all the madness"* for without that relationship with God we can never be at peace. We can never be whole. Don't be fooled, we need that relationship with God so when the madness around us began to swallow us, we can call out to the father and know that his mercy and grace will gently flow upon us. We were given that right when God the father gave his only begotten Son Jesus upon the cross in a time in which the madness was new in the world.

Weeping Tears

Weeping Tears is a poetic expression that came upon me as I was watching a PBS special about the soldiers who are fighting in the Iraq war. I felt overwhelmed when one of the stories about a platoon of soldiers who were ambushed and many of these soldiers were very young and their platoon commander was much older. He had always wanted to make sure that every man who was out on a run with him would return. On this particular day it didn't work out that way. When the day was over, this commander found himself lying to a soldier whom he knew was dying because of his injury. He had to boost the soldier up telling him he was alright and everything was okay when in fact it was not.

At some point during this segment this commander wept. He didn't mind shedding the tears. He felt hurt for the families of these young soldiers who would have to face the terrible reality from the messengers telling them their son or daughter has died. War is madness, but even in times of such tribulation we must hear God over all the madness.

Weeping Tears

Tears we weep in time of sorrow
Tears we weep in time of happiness
Tears we weep in time of pain
Tears we weep in fortune and fame
I cry tears for the fallen soldier
I cry tears for the wounded innocent
I even cry tears for the enemy
Even in woe and infamy
Tears ever so useful
Will often heal the fearful
I pity the one who cannot cry
For their soul must be ready to die
Weep not for me
Weep not for you
But weep for this world
So long overdue

Daughters In Christ I Prayed for You

My inspiration for "Daughters in Christ I prayed for you" was merely my way of recognizing the many beautiful young ladies in our congregation whom I have had the pleasure to watch their spiritual growth. I see them come and go. Some have chosen to stay in the fellowship of our wonderfully blessed church and others, well have chosen to leave. Some have chosen a ministry that will enhance their young lives and others are just there to catch the eye of our very young and dynamic pastor. For whatever their reasoning I was inspired to pray for them. I hope that when that day in which they experience the madness to come. For now they are young and curvy and got it going on. When that day comes when they begin to loose the luster of good looks, curvy body and "things just not going on" I can only pray and hope they will have filled their hearts with the Godly word imparted to us by the man of God. It will be important to have a relationship with God so that they too will be able to Hear God over all the madness.

Daughters in Christ I Prayed for You

To my daughters in Christ
Yes, you! Sweet and charming ebony Queens
I prayed for each of you
Asking God to render to you,
Your needs first and then your wants.
Though, it may seem our ages do not match
For you may want this and I may want that
Make no mistake, or take for granted
God's gonna reward you from the seeds you planted.
Whether you are a mother, or a daughter, a wife or a sister,
Without a doubt God will bring you out.
God in all his Glory, has written our life story
So rest assured and walk in peace
God will give you his perfect peace
I prayed for you my daughters in Christ
Yes, you! Sweet and charming ebony Queens

I Miss You Mom

"*I Miss You Mom*" is a poem I wrote in memory of my Mother, Mrs. Sarah Barham. My mother was a tiny woman full of love and compassion. She along with my father raised three children. It was that love that we got from them that helped my siblings and I enjoy what we have gained in our lives today. They taught us the value of a quality life. I can never forget the moments I would see my mother reading her bible and she would often write down her thoughts. I believe she heard the voice of God even in all the madness that she would later in life experience. She was like the woman in Proverbs 31. I know my siblings will agree with me that Mom was the major glue in our family. Mind you, our Dad Arthur W. Barham, was a great Dad and he and Mom had the kind of love and respect for one another that showed us how to respect one another. They made sure that we were well provided for. Looking back, I cannot remember a time in which we were ever without food or decent clothing. As an adult I can now look back and just be in awe over how Mom and Dad made ends meet and provided for us on their income. Granted we were not rich. We didn't live in the best houses or go to the finest schools or experience the every summer vacations. . We learned how to be grateful for even the smallest things. We had more than the material things; we had pure love from our parents and grandparents. Those were the village keepers that helped mold us into the persons we are today. My brother Arthur and my sister Alice and I were not smothered to death, meaning they (especially Mom) gave us some rope to venture out (*with instructions mind you*) and taste a little of the world. It was from those special times that we could come back and ask questions and get answers. I will always have the memory of my mother and father in my heart and mind. "*I miss you Mom*" was an expression in recognition of her last day on earth. I remember it was the day before mother's day 2002 and it was on a Saturday morning. I was getting ready to go the hospital to visit her. I thought I would take the time and make a happy Mother's Day banner to go over her bed. As I was waiting for the colorful banner to finish printing, I received a phone call from my sister-in-law Lucy. Her voice sounded low and somewhat trembling. I greeted her and in the next phrase she told me that Mom had passed. I just didn't know what to say or do. It was an emptiness that I will never be able to describe. Right then every moment

I had of my mother flashed within my mind. There were happy and sad moments. Of course I headed on over to the hospital. I had not yet cried, I was sad but not to tears. Was there something wrong with me? I asked myself. Was I relieved about Mom's death? I didn't really know what I was feeling. God please be with me was what I was chanting during my ride to the hospital. When I arrived at the hospital and walked into her room, I met my brother Arthur and sister-in-law Lucy. I saw my mom lying in bed as if asleep. She had on a pink gown and her hands were clutching a pink carnation. She looked so peaceful and had a smile of contentment. That is when I cried. That is when I knew this was real. Later that day I learned from my brother that mom was having her breathing treatments and some how her breathing became more laboring. As the technician was working on her mom began started focusing her attention on the TV. At that time a well-known minister was preaching and according to my brother mom was in deep concentration on his message. As he began his crescendo within his sermon that is when mom took what my brother described as a very long and deep breath, her last breath. Upon hearing this I knew Mom was hearing the voice of God over all the madness. She was diagnosed with Alzheimer's disease a new word for dementia. Truly that was moms madness, but yet somehow as she ended her life she heard Gods voice over the madness. I do remember that about two weeks before she passed I had a quiet moment with her in the nursing home, it was that moment I will always believe in my heart the moment she and I said good-bye. Without speaking as I was feeding her, I began to cry (something I had said I would never do in her presence) tears. She looked into my eyes and her eyes became watery yet she didn't say anything. I know deep down she wanted to hug me and say it is all right like she would do when we were little and would hurt ourselves, she would always comfort us. I found myself saying to her, I love you Mom you have been a great mother and if you are tired it was okay to rest. She had this little sheepish grin on her face as if she was saying; "I know something you don't know." I didn't know that I was saying my good-byes to her then. Perhaps it was during that moment she was hearing God over all the madness.

I Miss You Mom

I miss you Mom so very much.
Your gentle, sweet and tender touch
Your warm and delicate quiet smile.
Prepared me for a life worthwhile
How little did I know
Our last time together would be.
Your gentle way of saying,
My soul is tired Lord, please release me.
On that faithful May Saturday morn
Your body weary, weak and worn.
As the preacher man shouted out his story
You lift your head and raised hands toward glory

It's Just Me, All Alone

I t's just me, all alone was inspired by my driving home on the interstate and I could not help but notice the make shift pallets and other debris lying under the underpasses of the bridge. Occasionally I would see the owners of the humble abode. I began to wonder what manner of lives did these people once have. What brought them to this condition? What was the madness that they could not escape? What drove them to live like this? Unfortunately I didn't take the opportunity to stop and ask. I guess out of fear. So I do not know if it was enough but I prayed for them each time I passed by. As I look back I really believe that they had inner peace. I also believe that the little community in which they had developed was probably a better one than our own structured neighborhoods. No doubt they probably looked out for one another; they probably knew each other's names and in spite of their humble means they probably were able to hear God over all the madness.

It's Just Me, All Alone

It's just me, all alone.
I am the homeless man under a bridge.
I am the child you did not want.
I am the lady, bags and all.
I am the burden in the nursing home.
Brother can you spare a dime.
I am Wednesday's child so full of woe.
Here's a bag; there's bag...
Without Medicaid or Medicare,
I'm neither here... nor there
It's just me all alone
As a child I was not homeless
Before I was born you wanted me
I use to bring the bags home and
Now my bags are my home.
It's just me, all alone.

My Permanent Friends

My Permanent Friends is an expression of love to my own brother and sister. I don't have to expound greatly about this it is self-explanatory. God was so generous to bless our parents with more than one child. Thus allowing us to have unconditional friends. Friends that in case the madness in each of our lives seems to overwhelm us we know we can at least count on that sibling to pray for strength. I can truly say that God has heard my cry of unity among my siblings and I. It was not always a safe place, but since hearing God over all the madness, God has allowed my siblings and I to become closer to one another. Thank you God for my permanent friends!

My Permanent Friends

(Dedicated to my Sister, Alice B. Stansberry and my Brother, Arthur C Barham with Love)
I have two permanent friends.
Who sticks with me through the end.
The love comes from our heart.
And with this we shall not part.
I know their favorite song.
I love them right or wrong.
I know they love me too.
To them I will be true.
To God we give him Glory.
O for such a life story.
I'd rather have none other.
Than my own, sister and brother.

In Conclusion

The expressions I have shared are just a few of many. I know that as God continues to inspire me I will be able to tell the good news that God is with us. Once we establish a relationship with God, we will hear his voice over all voices. There will not be anything that will keep us from his love, that agape love that binds us as one. I know I am hearing God over all the madness. His voice is so sweet and soothing. When I lost my job, it was God's voice that said not to worry. In my times of uncertainty for my life, it is God's voice that lets me know that he can restore in me a clean heart. A renewed heart!

I want everyone who has doubts about anything, to know that as long as we keep God first in our lives, he will take care of you and hearing God over all the madness will become easier and easier. After all God is with us. He is in our hearts!

My Prayer

Father God; thank you for allowing me to see yet another day; A day that does not belong to me. Thank you God for your love and concern over my life; I realize there is nothing I have done so great, that warrants you to keep me daily! Thank you God for allowing me to reach someone who may have needed to know about you. God I thank you for being you and having your grace and mercy ready to dispatch on my behalf. Father God thank you for all you have done in my life and all I know you will continue to do in my life. Father I bless your name. Father God in all my endeavors may you be the head. God I thank you in advance for taking charge of my life and mold me to be the better person you would have me to be. I know I have sinned and have fallen short of the glory. I also know that you are a forgiving God. I will forever thank you for your untiring mercy and grace, here now and forever, Amen.

Printed in the United States
54826LVS00001B/55-60

9 781425 927929